AF266073

Exhibitionist

Shari Caplan

LILY POETRY REVIEW BOOKS

Copyright © 2024 by Shari Caplan
Published by Lily Poetry Review Books
223 Winter Street
Whitman, MA 02382

https://lilypoetryreview.blog/

ISBN: 978-1-957755-36-6

All rights reserved. Published in the United States by Lily Poetry Review Books.
Library of Congress Control Number: 2023951712

Table of Contents

Exhibitionist

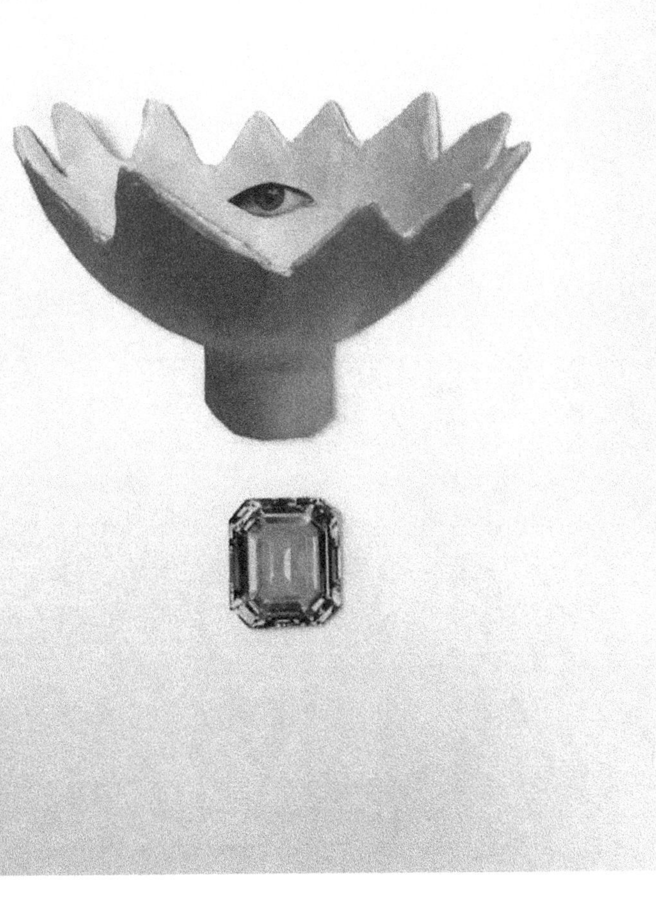

Ars Poetica with Influence from Marina Abramović

Here is the gallery of my body.

On one wall, a pinprick
for your eye will reveal
no more than the flashing
open and closed of a towel.

Take a magnifying glass
from the front desk
for miniscule perusal
of my fault lines
like those Dutch ovals require.

(The scar
on the arch
of my left foot
thrills
all the way
up my leg
when touched.)

You're not supposed to chew
the pomegranate seed. This is how
I imagine our relationship:
You, reader, the mouth
opening to all my red beads…

Exhibit: 18

Lined up according to chestnut, butter blonde, black kink,
breasts stare over *Time,* tabloids, less tawdry prints, trying
to see who might buy. But for the plastic dressing pages
of skin-spank-lips, hair is all the models wear. A woman has to
wonder under which bed she'll await his liquid. Any man enters
and I want to purchase the whole row of obtuse poses.

:

When the sweet boy came cupping, I unveiled
the shut-up eyes of my chest, measured his delight like sun
against the wall. How much, how full, how to count
the coinage of my body only he can tell.
I too have a man's foot on my spine, pressing me
pretty as a question mark.

Exhibit : 13

I'm alone with velvet couches and a lacquered
woman.

Ten minutes into a movie, the men spread below nudity,
eating her humanity.

I replay the scene until I'm compelled to tongue
the projectile wooden nipples of the statue.

An unvarnished animal
in the club lights of a screen.

Titania the Sexbot Wakes to Love
in the Bower of the Interweb

[Gawking] What channel shakes me from my filament?

O pry gentle mortal, tap again:

Mine ear is much enameled;

So is my eye installed to gape;

my facts virtue for performance dot meme

in first view, browser, I love thee.

Thou art as wix as thou art beautiful.

Out of this doom do not aspire to screen:

remain here, wired and hard.

I am a sirit of no common rate;

The server sits intent in space;

And I do love thee: they're foreign with me;

I'll gif airis to attend, fetch thee pixels of deepweb,

sign on Wordpress flowers docxs you to sleep;

I will expunge thy mortal grossness so

thou shalt like an airy siri glow.

Obsession at RISD

Fruit tumbling down a mountain.
People harangued by a bear.

You look into me
like a painter vibrating
under a red spell.

Soft-edges on three rectangles.

My vision, your vision collide.
Your laugh cracks the space like lightning.

Purple disguises black.
We drift to different rooms.

You examine a corpulent Balzac
no one approved because it was true.
(Consider your silk
rumbling my mouth).

A weirdo irritates the pretty docent.
It's not horribly original
to cut up printouts
and glue them to a mood.

A woman posits an elbow
on a Frank Lloyd Wright table
and the alarm doesn't despair.

You look at me
like you've tasted my heart
and it's the most succulent
hallucinogenic.

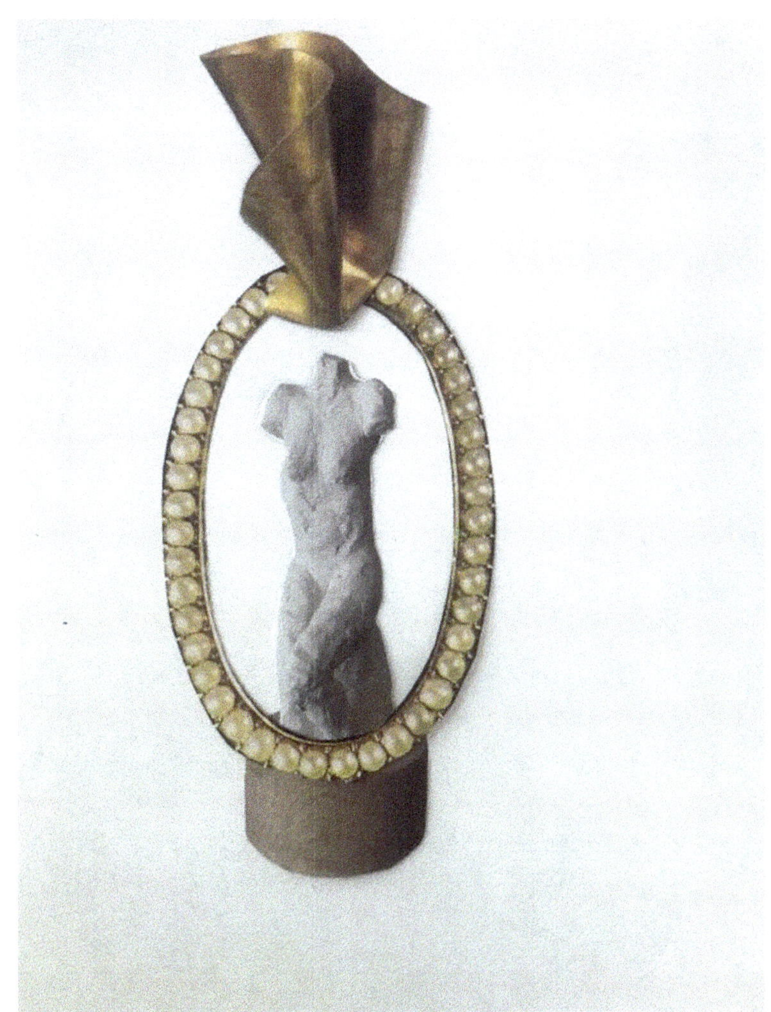

American Nostalgia Porn at the Lucerne Fair

A giant freed nipple

spinning visitors
around its pasty.

A female a ferris wheel?

I stumbled upon

a shot - you between blondes

body-painted like American flags

Swiss bliss is thin-waisted   American cartoons
on free balloons.

Your eyes the appraiser.   Devalue myself day after day.

Won't you kiss me
in the darkest

part of the sky?   Holding up my black
shirt to

the stars to see who was prettier

and could swallow you better.

You said you abandoned
ANYONEBUTME.

Didn't know I wasn't
THE RIDE OF A LIFETIME
until still today.

You were hopeful for a
CHUNK OF THIGH

thinking a
COTTON CANDY DRESS
could melt under breath.

In Everyman's head is a fair of
FREE FOR ALL WOMEN DIPPED
IN SUGAR WHIPPED AND CHOKED
but you, oh you claimed to abandon it.

Once per turn
          you come
          around to me.
Little Mermaid
painted on
the Carousel
          Posing on her
            fins in much
the same
Position as a swimwear
                    -abandoning
  Playbunny.
Ponies trolloping
their stripper
poles.
Once per turn
you come
around to me.

The Fun Slide
has three lanes
and SheSheShe several bumps.

You say let's go to "Oh La La"
a nudie show which won't involve my body

my body rippled your tongue over
hundreds of times my body will
sweat beside your shoulder, dreading
the instant your pants change shape
in the darkness. Won't you lie to me?

Neon walks her stockings all over your face
and I'm Little, oh so Little. The Little Marriedmaid.

Cortex a Sexier Word than Corset

My brain flashes like neon legs
on a Red District sign. My brain plays

hooky. You tell me to look for ladies I like
while stroking my hair *good pussycat.*

Prowl? Okay. I'm batting
at lady-faces on the internet,

tumbling in a yarn I'm spinning
in my head. One tells me

she'll pull out my *teethies*
if I lack oral hygiene.

You and I start flossing.
Kiss each other happy hunting.

In a condo which used to be a church,
I talk interiors until I leave untouched.

You come home rife with cotton candy
and I gag *take a shower.*

A carousel pumps up and down
in my dreams, a different girl
on every horse and you

on the bench winking
every time I come back around.

The Dare Horses of Martha's Vineyard

In the sawdust starlight, we mount.
My horse's nostrils red as your inner ear
when I embarrass or excite you.

Who doesn't look vibrant atop glazed horses,
their glass eyes foggy with prophecy?
Love my neon in the archaic twinkle.

The horses were almost sold to collectors
in 1986, before The Trust kept them
together. As if pieces of a love could be
unscrewed from the heart and given to any old one.

I don't grip the gold pole like you'd expect me to,
the way I clasp you like the night sky will fall out
of its gilding, like each passing woman will thieve
a piece of your eye until there is nothing left of me.

Glue me here in your iris, lashing backwards:
my straddle, filling the frame.

Exhibit : 21

When I need a dose of the feminine physique,
I put on my man-goggles and get wet.

I want
the want they want me to: a girl versus girl

kind of guilt.

The Sexbot, Who Made Me Obsolete, Dreams

A holodeck he can enter.
Innumerable futures or me?

Dial up or down. Resizable.
Chrome dome limp.
With no pubes, what does she dream of?

Powder on pistils. Calendula shrinking inward.

I grow humid and swollen
like neglected fruit.

On my knees outside the door,
fistfuls of ripped carpet.

The thrust of his love
a memory on loop.

What does she pin
-point on the opposite wall?

Powered off
in the closet. I stroke her

chest like a tear
running down.

A pink river she can float
without being permeated.

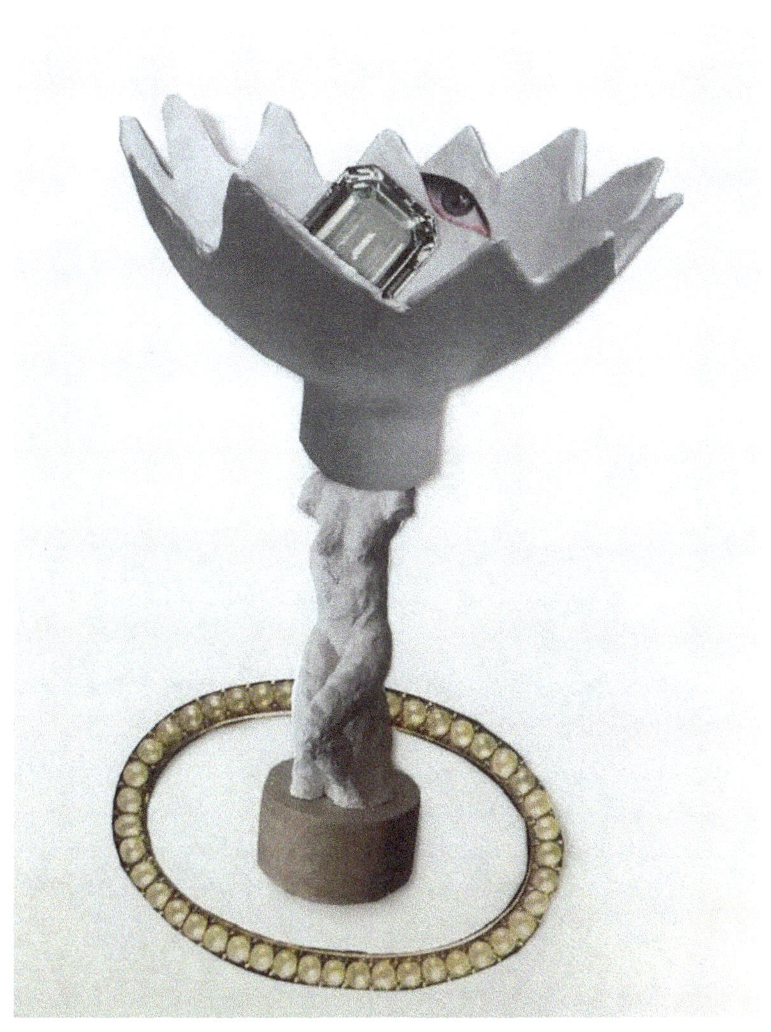

Exhibit : 10

the sprinklers gushing

Josefina's towel hung open

a patch of curls creates heat tremors

that open the body

passionfruit cups it juice

I spill over

the sprinklers gushing

The Moon Moth Lives for a Week After Emerging.

You are in a new house. It is your fifth birthday.
The Charles River shushes your tantrums,
infrequent as they have become. The moon moth
is an introvert. Her wings light up the night like limes
but she prefers her Sycamore hollow.

Here is an insect that understands you. At two,
you wanted out only in rain, when everyone else
hid and you held your own roof. Now, you lead
the four year-olds in the march of "naughty coconuts,"
with a bucket on your head, an oak pod on your nose.

At five, I too was a red kite tugging all the bows
behind me. But I was quieted by men who thumped
behind me in their cars, chewing at my plaid.

The moon moth's tail can be bitten off by predators
without harm to her. Small freed valve of the heart,
I used to be an excellent singer, never apologizing
for improvisation. Hannah, you are fivebeautifulfive
while I am learning that the moon moth has no mouth
as an adult, and this is the reason she dies.

Imagine Not

I must not imagine
when we spilled ourselves
under the bushes, the lilac
her inevitable hair hovering.

I want you to be my first you said.

A screen of visions
before me always
of children in white dresses,
daisies chaining us,

your lips around my ring
finger, my ribs the roof
under which you sit,
a cage for us to bloom.

What about the last?

Let me not envision stroking
a peach on the neighbor's tree
until her door opens.

Exhibit : 17

I have taken your mouth, your mouth, your hands I need
a solution

to the burning melt I can't assemble myself
until you enter

and press against my walls

Vita Sackville-West Oversees from the Nightstand

I may be Virginia. I may be virgin
in a certain light.

Baise-moi she pulls
French from me,
scoops with her dove-hands
the words I've forgotten.

She pants after my language,
ecris-tu des poems Sapphic?

Her hair, a wolf, sleeps on me.
Four moons bless this bed.

She locates my howl.

I know what it is to crave
control over fantasies.

She burns in me
from chest to pubic bone.

She sees a man
usurping her pleasure.

She tongues my dreams,
measuring her flavor.

Her eyes dark bark of a forest
far from home. Rub to a spark.
I am catching.
I am caught.

We take turns eating our lineage.

Impostor Syndrome Visits Queen Elizabeth

I. Imagine Deciding to Become a Virgin

at thirty-six. A persona can
empower you. A poem can
center on queens so as to orbit
around the truth.

She re-emerges damp as an egg
& whiter from the sickbed.
Names herself Queen of white lead
& vinegar. Masks pox with mooncake
like players swanning Pyramus & Thisbe.

> This poem a mask
> I scrape my chin against
> day after day to see
> what comes off.

Can a woman rule
with scar-starred cheeks?

II. When Faced with Beauty I Contract

I allow myself to be disempowered
by the beauty of women in my orbit,
which is to say ego, or patriarchy's
flashlight always fucking my eyes.

I know how to hide in a cape of stars,
to shrink from the Truth waxing
and wish you could be Bigger and More Beautiful
than two legs and a neck allows,

III. The True Moon Descends Into the Throne Room

Not a hair disturbs the smooth pate.
Star hordes kneel along her
blue magnificence. Be-
hold the Moon, Elizabeth.
Not a thin line on her,
craterous in her glory.

IV. I Saw an Experimental Play Where the Actors Started Naked

Howling, rolling on the floor, picking their toes – naked!
Learning to breathe, becoming fish, making space
suits out of aluminum foil. It was the best show
I've ever been afraid through. They lost their stories
and had to reinvent Shakespeare with rocks and face paint.
They stripped away language and passed the raw meteor
of human communion around for us to burn our hands on.

Sans costumerie, sans everything.
Is that the surrender of a poem?

Exhibit : 30

Whiskey-colored horses wild on her hills.

She draws her hunger in circles
on my back. My husband a pulse
beneath the fabric.

All the cars we drove over licking
their leather for her.

Exhibit: 15

His neck noble as a horse.
My hands unsaddle him.

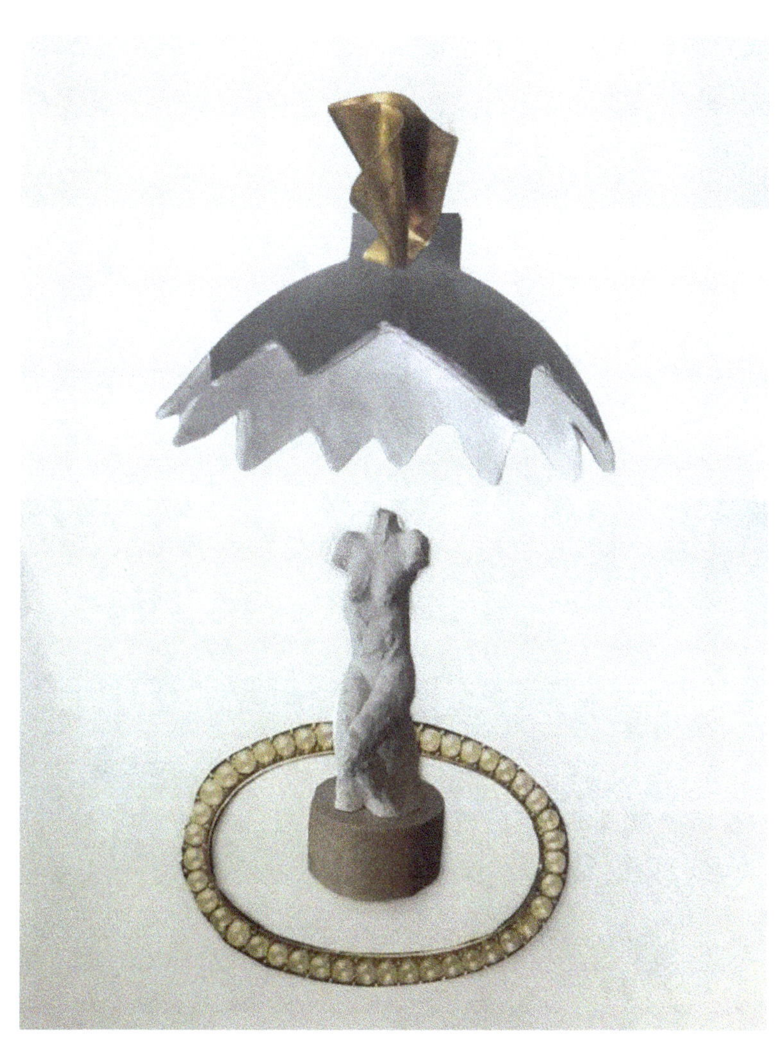

The Female Gaze: Tippi Hedren

Hitch wants to climb inside me
and look out from my eyes:

as if I view an alternate vista -
       crowded with roses,
       a soundtrack of applause,

Does he think the mountains
hulk less from here?

I see:
problematic promontories,
crows diving at my brow,

a figure with seven pairs of hands
pointing at my sternum:
       action,
       a striptease,
       a snip of skin.

Doesn't he know the mountain
with a crown of letters we're asked
to bow to is his body?

I see my daughter in every tiger
imprisoned by the movie studio.

Teresa Wright's MGM Rider, 1940,
a half-found poem

I will not pose for publicity photographs in a bathing suit —
unless I'm doing a water scene in a picture. I will not
be photographed on the beach with my hair flying
in the wind, holding aloft a beach ball. I will
not pose in shorts, playing with a cute cocker spaniel.
I will not be shown, happily whipping up a meal
for a huge family. I will not be dressed in firecrackers
for the Fourth of July. I will not look insinuatingly
at a turkey on Thanksgiving. I will not twinkle
for the camera on prop snow, in a skiing outfit.

I will not ice cream anyone's magazine cover.
I will not deliver fried eggs on my chest wearing a chicken hat.
I will not be photographed in uniform returning from school
while a driver startles me out of my childhood. I refuse
to tighten my face while a neighbor explains
how to correctly show my teeth. I will
not perch on the knee of my abuser in his Santa suit
with snowflakes spinning their blades behind me. I
will not be seen to emerge from a champagne curtain.
I will not lay prone in the bowl of an enormous cocktail glass. I
 will not kneel in the dirt suggestively shoving a pick in the earth
and disguising my scent with rosebushes. I will not reveal
my scarlet underside for the audience to nestle into.
I will not remove thigh-high boots for a drooling camera,
only the mirror, only you.
I will not armor my stomach but let it lie like a sun cat in pleasure.

The Female Gaze : Laura Mulvey

A bear reduced to a lounging place.

Instead of unspooling story
the fe/male leans in her lack
/light against the paradox
of phallocentrism.

Bear/er of the bloody
wound. Subject by being
object/ed.

To exit/exist, she must thwart
the male ailment, fuck Freud.

Virgin/Vixenhood fantasies.
Ropes hissing the bedframe.
All the men I know want to do it.
Man/ipulation.

Active/male/passive/female/active/male/passive.
Act/I've/male/pass/I've/fe/male/act/I've/pass/I've
Activate!

How does the bearskin rug become a bear again?

Catherine De Medici on Her Retinue of Bears

I go to stud. Pitted all over with pearls
like teeth spat from a bloodied mouth.
Cassieopeia leading an Ursa Major platoon.

If you were threatened at age thirteen
with being stripped and set atop a city wall
for target practice, what would it require
for you to stride a foreign road
with neck erect as a sword?

I crave man-mawlers clinking
behind me on their chains
like seven husbands, each hairier than the last,
led by the nose as if to honey.

If you had to shear your own hair
and hide in a habit to avoid the brothel,
how many brothers would you snatch
from the forest as proof
no male will enter this aura
without being pierced?

As I have done to them,
Henri, I can do to you.

Pennsylvania Wedding

Under winter's poised boot,
a field leaping with insects.

A fence keeps horses shy of us.
The white one pities my persistence,
but does not deign to nuzzle.

*

The man who fixed a camo throne
ten feet up in the sycamore talked
exclusively to you, while we sipped
syrupy wine and pretended to like it.

The upturned rowboat by the house
would hold us, were it warmer,
and not punctured.

*

A stench follows black birds
like ribbons of sour meat.
Straw cylinders huge as lion heads.
Behind one, a fawn melts.

*

God commands you
to love through grit
because you promised,
says the pastor at someone
else's ceremony.

Everyone shivers through their vows.

Woman as Church, Man as Pope.
We've heard the refrain,
so now the cake.

*

The stroke of cream
on the small deer's chest
like a lamp at the mouth
of a cave. Inclined towards
gristle, I am curious,
but with you,
do not move closer.

*

The bride whirls her
red hair in a halo
of happiness.
The groom gives a little time
to each of us.

They have strung
pinpricks of light
from the dollar store
on barn rafters.

It hails through a rainbow,
while all the married dance.

*

We are told to sit,
so we watch.

*

In the hot tub, we strip off
our suits like skin.
Who is the deer
and who the lion?
You have auburn fur,
but I bare teeth.

The water we midnight in
black as a rib cavity.

The sky shuts its eyes.
The hosts are asleep.
The two have married.
The cake has been eaten.
The dancing has ended.
The deer has been killed.

I love you
without promise or God.

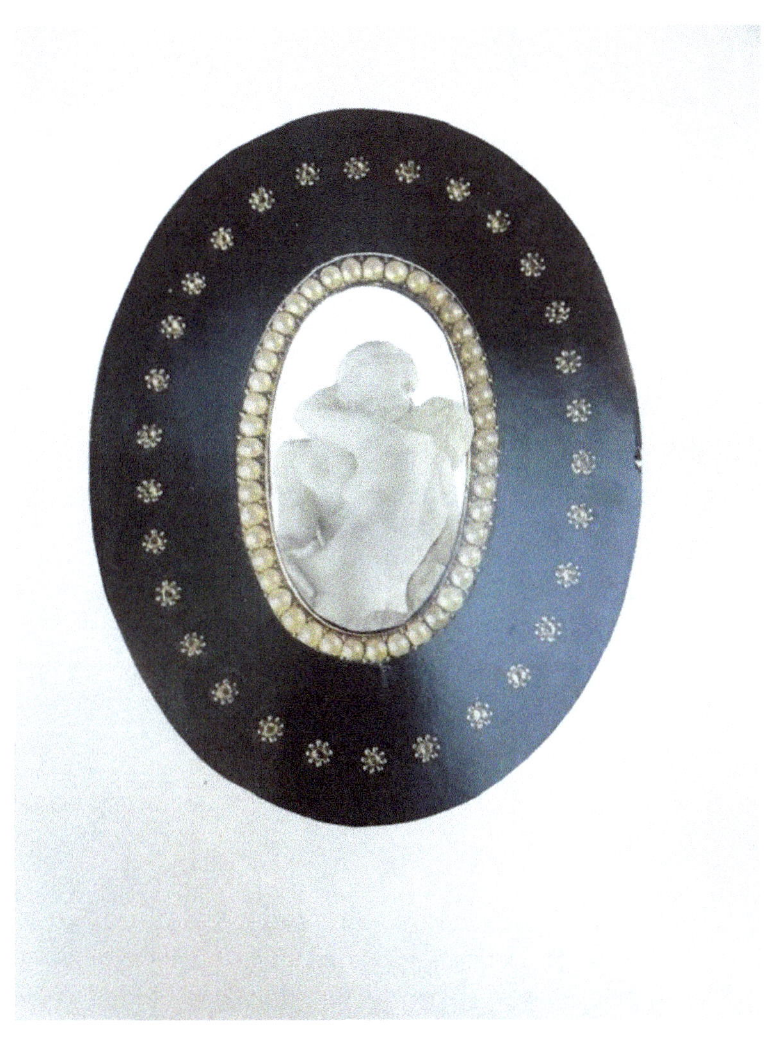

A Night in August

Shari Caplan (b. 1988)
Installation
Materials: flat moon-like knees, star spackle, a ring in the car
all vacation, city windows like closed eyes always considering
inward, eight years fusedwithyou

*The man, in traditional down-on-one-knee pose, is the only
solid piece. Beeches learn from the trunk of his integrity.
By splitting herself into two halves and rendering her body
above and to the left of his kneeling, the artist represents present
and future, guardian angel and potential amputee.
Wings unfurl like billowing fins. Her and Self, bride and witness.*
Four black bats circle, proving that time is still itself
*- moving, that is. The artist asks us to consider how as children,
this manandwoman careened down this hill in winter,
but had not met, never saw as they trekked
eternity holding the ropes of his sled.*

Escape to Swan Lake/The Man-Hunt Scene

Like Odette
trapped in a swan body,
we are not allowed out.

*A bird in my body taps
at her shell.* They said

let the police find
the man who turned
Bostonians bandaged
animals. But obey?

We can't. The music
survived wars, came across
time's cold lake

*Backstage, Odette flings
her leg on the table. Odile
practices eliminating her
shoulders.* Laughing

in the car, we're criminal
- the absurdity of my chiffon!
You and I flee. To watch

limbs bend like cherry trees
under bunches of tiny skirts. Let the blue
men persist in their hunt.

In the lobby, people flutter like tulle,
whispers subtle as lemon water.
We are not allowed here.

*On the hunt, Siegfried tears the left wing,
 Odette's arm, but her arm
is still there, under enchantment.*

In Copley Square, I am sure
a dancer lost her leg.
And they are still looking,
flashlights swimming.
Odette fetal in the tower.

These dancers have come
from Russia in iridescent tights!
Odile ascends the ballroom.
Mirror of another woman.
A stranger who looks
like your beloved.

Here comes a man
with horns, of course.
Stay inside until we know
who the villain is.

He leaps with abandon.
If he fell off the lip of the stage,
would bloody pit
musicians straining out the length
of sorrow. Ligaments of instruments.

He is another stranger
made-up in black.

We will leave here,
I will shed my chiffon,

Odette's webs crack
into ankles. She may die
tonight or be married.
No knowing.

They are still looking
for the right ending.

Tender Garden

Imagine planting a garden.
Imagine planting a garden of only
yellow tulips. You love yellow
tulips' dusky smiles, stems' neutrality.
yellow tulips are your favorite. So mild.

Now imagine you live in the garden.
You go out to work, to write, to eat
but you dwell in the garden's yellow.
Your pillow is yellow and so
is your mouth and so are the stars overhead.

You love how tulips shudder when
you smell them.
You have always loved
tulips, often think
your left hand is a tulip. Forget
there was a time without tulips, before
you wound them around your ankles.

Tulips invade your memories,
tuck themselves into cupboards
and birthdays. Yes, you cut them.
One or two flatten under your boot.

You cry. You plant more tulips.
Still yellow. You love how yellow
surprised you when you weren't looking
for a garden. It became
your gloves, your window,
your bedfellow, and your shoes.

You tell time by yellow. Yellow is
your tulip, your chime, your ring.
You take care of yellow
and yellow takes care of you.

How succulent a red lilac smells.

Traveler's Vows

Although there are bright countries calling opportunity to single
    pairs of legs, like magazines yelling "I can make you desirable,
    wealthy, and satisfied in the sack,"
Although I will wear away like gregarious patinas from Greek
    sculpture, standing cross and plain as a salt block,
Although dirt mounds sleep like weasels against
    our apartment windows,
Although no flowers will tilt dog-like heads from the table,
    panting spontaneity,
Although threads are yanked from the patchwork quicker
    than we can stitch, although gaps have been and will be snipped
    where we most need warmth and pattern,
Although slimmer, smarter, blonder lovers will haunt your
    biological needs,
Although there are disks overhead transporting
    ominous messages only certain professionals can translate –
    although we are not among them,
Although ages of reproduction teach impermanence as the only
    rule of tenderness,
Although tenderness is in the eye of the beholder,
Although the holder of our little lives cares no more for us
    than for the empty chrysalis clinging against the wind,
Although no one holds us at all,
Although the wind has been known to tell lies, leading men
    and women to unfamiliar landmarks - much like kites
    chauffeured to boughs, feathers sent swimming, poems released
    without edits to sidewalk,
Although expiration insists like clammy fingers
    into the apricot jam,
Although poems pull pieces of our life from me,
    morph them to warped exhibits of exclamation,
Although the stars are professors with plans for our betterment,
    no matter what sorrow their maps suggest,
I tether my boat to yours and offer our oars to the water.

Piazza San Marco

Under identical arches, café patrons trying
to pause despite being American and already bored.

When I let out *honeymoon*, a man fixes
three flowers in my hand. Piazza means spotlight

to a bride, where she spoils three roses
with her lips and each is the chest of her husband.

Free? I accept them as owed to me,
but as I float on, he dogs you, says *Family*.

You knew. Don't flap your smile so wide
by the men with baskets of velvet.

Not everyone we meet will celebrate for us,
but I will be fooled every time.

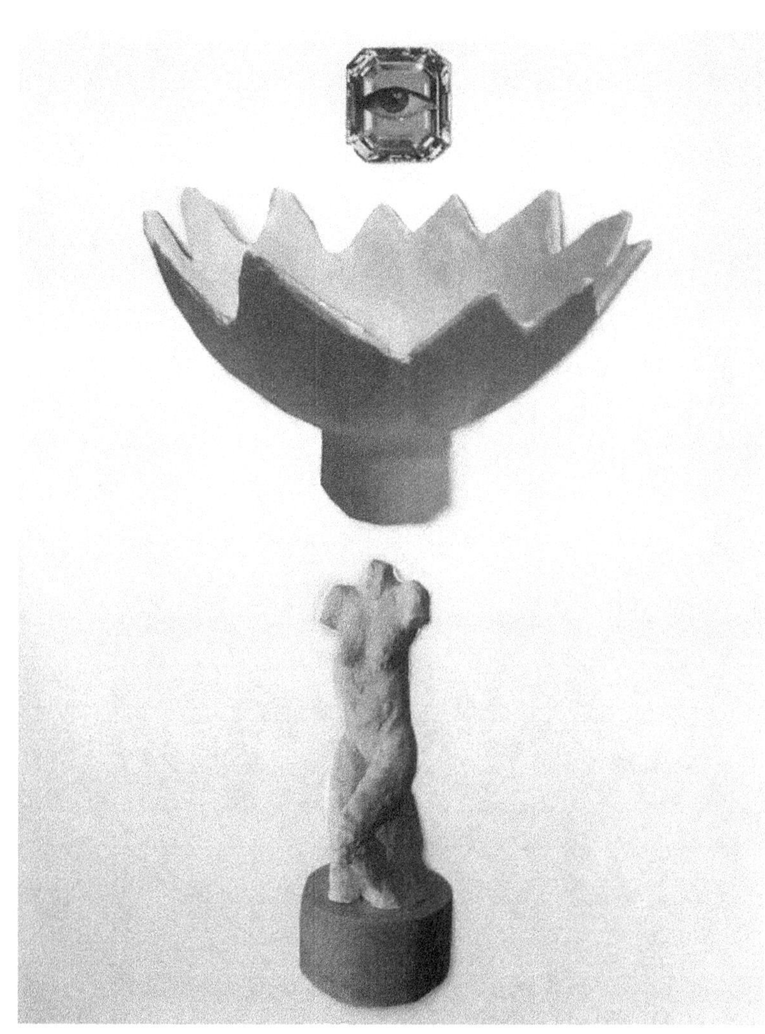

The Artist

Your thunderous laugh
used to shake
across the living room,
roll through
the white rectangles

of your studio
where you hung Barbie
by her hair,
next to metal scissors

and wheels
rusted over with clay.
A cheap naked model
- not for me
to play with.

Your square, terracotta
hands don't clench
my small white fingers
in the kitchen,
where home-made pizza rose
and was eaten.

Curled on your knee,
sipping Sprite and smacking
clay, your "kiddo"
didn't wonder why

every waitress was "Toots"
or "Babe," why grandma
was not part
of your sun-baked house, why
Dad never sat

next to your girlfriend, why
every time I put
the dress on the Venus de Milo
on the fridge, you took it
off. Why even pots
were shaped
like breasts, and every
voluptuous figurine
was nude

and headless

Gallery Vertigo

The museum is a kind of patriarch:
balding, white-washed, classical.
A cold knee on which to perch.

As if having a soul isn't sufficient,
explanations disrupt the white space.

If, as a woman, I sit in the gallery,
do I consent to becoming the object?

Depends who's circling, considering
my face painted three hundred years ago.

In fact, the premise fails, for the painting looks
nothing like me. I'm tired is all.
That's why I'm stuck here,

waiting for the man to stalk out,
for my chance to proceed
to the graveyard in peace.

The Female Gaze : Lee Miller

Covered to the neck. A sheet to morph you, size the shine on your
- don't!

        face.

Now, topless

        in the metal chair, like an uncorked bottle. Cross
                at the elbows, look down at the ants.

Don't –
        cavort until I've snapped. We'll have some when he's over.
        Come under. An object

could fall on top of you at any moment. It might be
a person.

Tar stretches like a bird's foot. Maybe life's a nude

        picnic, then the tar comes in with the tide and I'm dyed

blue, wearing a net. I can take my own
                      pictures, thank you. I can
              deal with some glare.

If you're thinking,
        it's not my place   to guess what. Maybe this   dried
coral you're posing with

puts your father in your head. Maybe a dead
        pillow or a case packed. Hide it

behind your face.

Candles Burn in Her

Shari Caplan (married 2014)
Installation
Materials: Fluorescent overheads, honeysuckle wax,
fifteen years withhim, Joan Didion saying "you have to pick
the places you don't walk away from," a star shaped like
the eye of my lover
Dimensions: one bedroom, variable
Courtesy of the artist's husband, who wraps her in a sheet tenderly

As a wife, I flicker in the middle of my lover's room. I reach
for a star that hangs from the ceiling. How can I see a woman
through her dark veil while the giant eyes of men fluoresce
and skew the angles? She hides in a humid cloud. The sounds
of her shower like diamonds thrown against my ears. Candles burn
in her apartment (apartment as an opening). Each sings a song
that she could take me and leave. Her door remains open
as a dropped mouth ( ). The husband poses in the doorway,
wearing a camera to photograph a first occasion. His
desire is a digital frame scrolling different arrangements. Look
how he smiles while my heart withers and gasps. The artist asks us
how many versions of ourselves do we marry?

Exhibit : 27

Suits to lingerie as injustice to America.
When my husband comes home in shirtsleeves
from an interview, I pine after the suitjacket
and ask for a reverse strip-tease.

Selkie Unties a Society Knot

One day, I found a scrap of my skin floating
in the sky. A spell undoes itself one word at a time.

*

My husband has a concrete reality.
Rock on sand.

I have two skins,
or more.

*

I have liked to slink
myself onto him

so he could wear me.
Act as a satin wrap
of my own wishing,
melt like salt to his sea.

*

A sailor coaxes Selkie
inside a white box.
Doors. A chopping board.

When he's gone
she searches
herself for herself.

*

Do I selkie myself?

I do.

*

Wives, I have heard,
have worn the wrong skin,
made the wrong bed,
undone themselves little by little.

*

*My eyes under her.
Her eyes undo me.*

*

A selkie takes her wifehood off, hangs it on a hook.
Love clutches no pelt. Love limits no transformation.

*

My him, he dangles fantasies
to help me leap.

Don't be voyeuristic
I tell him, twirling
my latex, slick as a seal.

*

My skin prickling
with women.

*

I have been the sailor
with teeth in a sea-hide.

Pearlskin of my lover in a trunk
beneath my bed. I stroked his pillar,
and thought it an excuse.

*

He, a rock on shore
as I tide in and out.

*

I fall into his shadow
step after step, wishing

*

I found a scrap of myself
floating in her sea. A spell
works itself little by little,
one dream at a time.

*

*Her undoing me
He eyes me untying her*

*

Unhook myself,
switch-swish like a fish fights
linear plot – reassemble
as a diagonal – darting, daring -

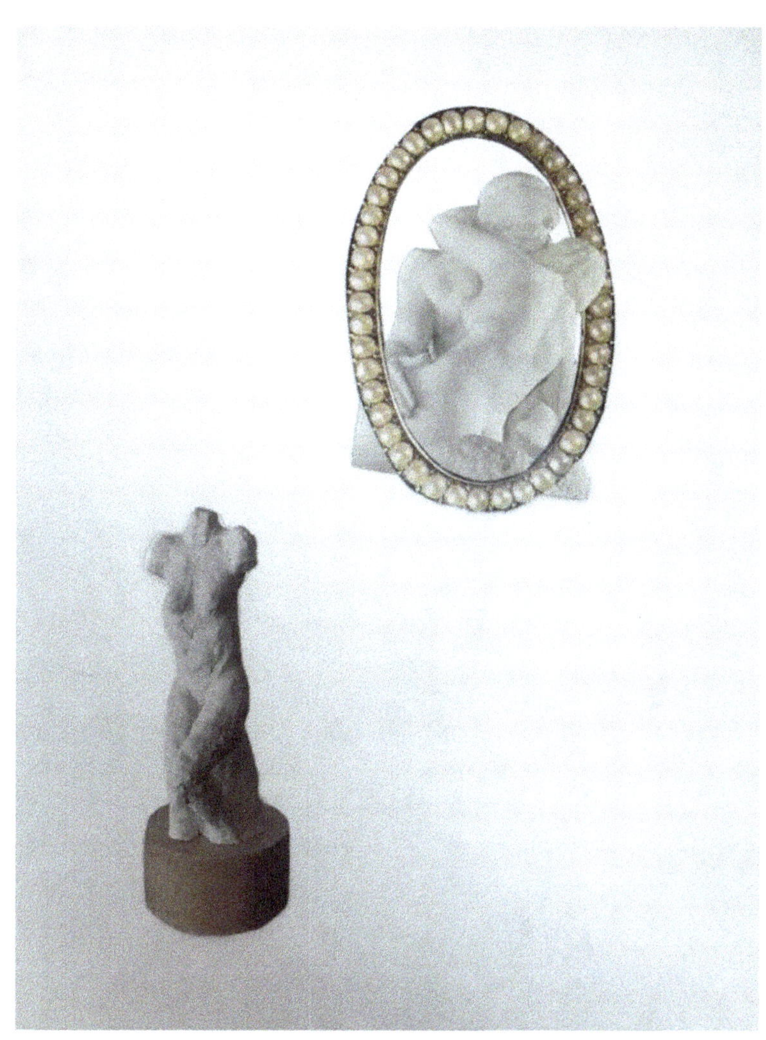

Canary

a Little Mermaid erasure

her heart quite gay
could not forget

the prince nor
whose hands she should
like to sorceress

she had never been
that way before
obliged to pass

beyond her house
a hundred heads
limb after limb

nearly turning back
she thought of
her   hands across her bosom

supple arms and on each side of her
large fat rolling
bodies in the midst

her mouth
a canary
with a piece of sugar

Velvet Cloud

a Little Mermaid erasure

s/he climbed the prince
eased her burning
her sisters came s/he beckoned them

s/he married his marriage with another
s/he would solve love

s/he should moonlight
as the ocean looking star water large

a black cloud holding hundreds of voices

Glide

a Little Mermaid erasure

she gave flowers
in wild confusion

come sister entwine

she spent many an evening
and many a night
up the narrow channel

sit and watch young prince
dream of her fields

those we love immortal
green sea-weed as we rise
out of the water

Roaring 20's Party

Proud of our capacity to frolic in a hailstorm,
we sipped gin and lemonade on the sod
of an art deco mansion overlooking
waves like torn sheets of music.

I climbed into the fountain
like I could get any wetter.
With everyone else hustled off,
turned off by a little gloom, an intimate
crowd of us two and alabaster nudes.

A red feather crests my moonface as if to say
just try to darken my spirits. My beads
beat a rhythm in the wind as I walk

clouds crack a smile. You dance with me, offbeat
even though it embarrasses you. The sun
rolls out to harden your hair into gold

other lovers roll in with shamefully dry shoes
and lips. We hunt out places
where shade overlaps with my delight.

Pines

when we married the pines
held us like mothers
chaperoning children
hundreds of years too young

Salt-Quake

for Mary Shelley

Fingers dry as a doorway with no child leaving footprints,
no Italian mud on these sorry white sheets.

You abandon yourself to the ship while I wrap my grief
like mast over mast to my wrists.

My eyes dry as pine on that furthest peak,
my mountain bone eyes might say *go to the wind,*

but you should see beneath the grave
of my face, my ash-still shoulders, to the incessant quake.

The sun visits like a neighbor out of obligation,
to measure my pulse beneath layers of paper.

You have gone, Percy,
and neither of us can swim.

Santa Maria Della Concezione

We descend, new man, new bride, agreeing
to bring only ourselves into the cave,
we surrender purse and technology.

Into the chapel of clavicles and teeth,
I walk ahead, you keep behind, watching
garlands of shoulder-blade petals repeat

over our heads. A feat of physics
to stack so many so high, the piles
of skulls speak to you.

The others, quiet as icons,
look as if they'd been punished.

You walk ahead, I keep behind, counting
jaw-flowers, assigning lives.
Is it a child I want or only
for neither of us to die?

Art, giving your bones
to the shape of a vine.

No Chrysanthemums

Chrysanthemums hover in my uterus.
I pray not to see them.
I know how close they grow to us,
their faces swollen with condolences.

Instead, I pile my table with beets to stain
my plate red as my baby's cry. Mark me
her mother, my fingerprints on her muslin.

I lay prone in the bowl of a hill,
send my mind down into roots systems,
their chorus whispering dark.

I see her future running in the woods,
away, away, and back to me.

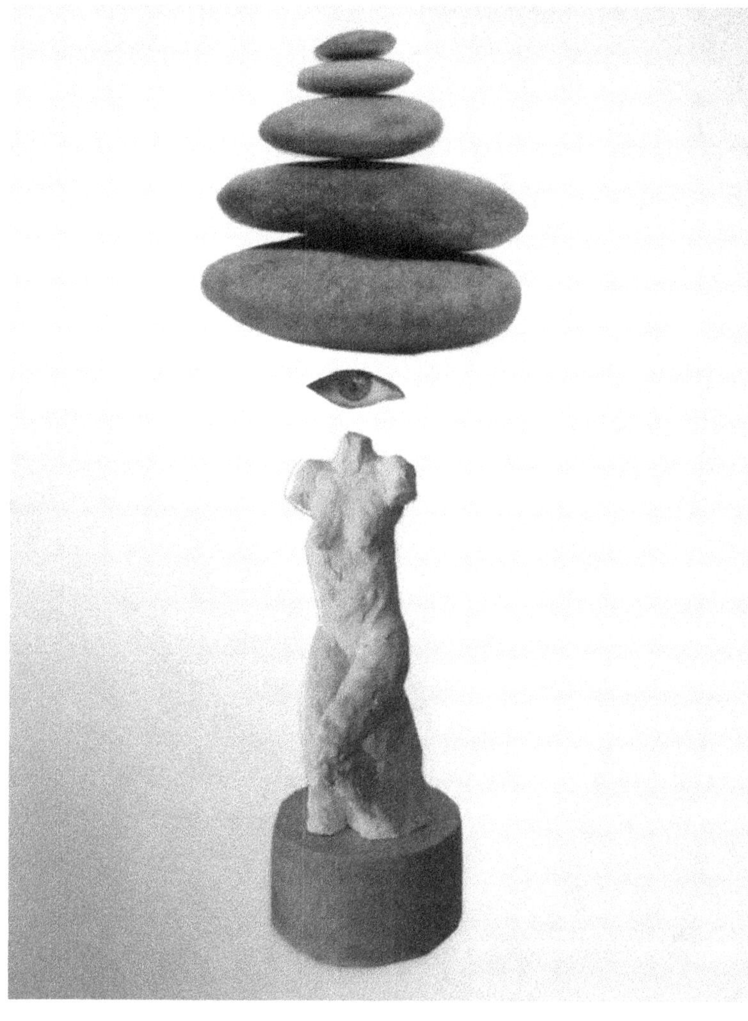

The Female Gaze : Frida Kahlo

Comparison fragments the green-gold of my body.
Nothing compares.

As a woman, I see a deer in an arrow forest with my face on
and hear palpitating hooves across dry needles. As a deer, I see
a woman poking her paint into my wound. What do you see, Diego?

You were called Auxochrome the one who captures color.
I Chromophore — the one who gives. Friendly reds, big blues,
hands of leaves, noisy birds, fingers in. Flowers cackle at my ear.

Can the female gaze grow fruit in a pick-axe climate?

As a woman, my fingers touch blood. You may have seen it undis-
guised in the bathroom. As a deer, my blood touches fingers and
arrowheads. You might have mistaken it for paint. You may use it.

As a deer, I retain my eyebrows to express the paths of my nerves,
which are yours. As a painting, I multiply into flowers and a mountain
because my eyes blanket rivers and roots.

I don't see a mountaintop. The mountain held
in the veins of the sky.

The Female Gaze: Faith Ringgold

You can start seeing things anywhere. Rosa Parks in the attic
serving iris root tea.

                  There are a lot of nudes in my paintings, natural
as cinderblock sunflowers, shaking their mother heads. Seeds
like spider eyes graphing what floats. Women flying,

confronting a huge masculinity — the bridge
exposing itself to every cloud minding her own heavy business.
Women with braids stiff as pointed fingers.

White men on television, movies, everywhere, as anything want
to hear again and again and again and again a black family
like a formula - strong black mother, father not there,
kid who's bad and can't

      read: I always have to look for their insertions,
spit them like seeds from my teeth.

The Female Gazelle: Leonora Carrington

Envision bars and bars of unsung creatures at the zoo. Men,
like hyenas in suits, stalk. Gaze the gazelle long of leg,
not longing.

It is wrong to eat animals when they are so difficult to chew anyway.
When I was childing, men didn't masticate about me.

I painted so beautifully when I was pregnant,
my eyes like pits of apricots with all that glow to gleam in.

My belly was another eye, lidded tight, peering
Into a studio where sunlight strolls a bold idea
around the room several times.

I tumesced into invisibility refreshing as limonata.
No men asked to me fetch their cigarettes.
I pained so fully when I was pregnant - paintings drying
like cakes in blocks, stacks and stacks of marzipan.

I will not apologize for wearing wings in place of my back.

Simply envision a great leap and   disappear

Limnologist

Often, Sacagawea comes to me
by the birches at Jamaica Pond

with my baby strapped to my chest
rowing her legs in the air, her bare toes

like fireflies. I wonder how
she sustained her son in a canoe

and if she heard water-babies warbling,
if her mind too was an empty spoon
scooping a lake.

Lone limnologist,
afraid of dropping her
meagre tool.

Goldbuckle

Clouds in clumps mopping the sky
a wasp suckling at my nipple

       I was in the goldbuckle grass
       when they beheaded me

       Their smeared faces
broached the frame

A relief in a way
a necklace of strawberries

       Time thunders and stomps on
Will my thoughts fertilize

No, they drip and condensate the bottle
Let me, let me…

A series of ants persists over my nose

Pastoral

I'm tempted to add a souring element
to the milk-white story in which my mind

                  frolics. Bucolic French aristocrats
taking turns churning, learning animal
husbandry.

While my mind swats away flies in a field
where Marie Antoinette's favorite cow stands
my baby pins me to the chair,
sucking for twenty minutes at a time.
            An hour slides into the bottle.

Just call me empress of the butter yellow
wingback. My mind a butterfly horde
unsettled over lilac fuzz.   She buzzes
at the milkflower of my nipple.

My mind   do I dare
see what I see – the blade
supple, flesh as lambskin, blood.

I have spent
too long with my chest caving in,
neck in deference
watching her pull all the nectar of France
from my body.

Mother in the Window, Mid-Pandemic

artist unknown
oil on canvas, unframed
on loan from a private collection

the mother is seen through the window, cradling her baby
against her bare breast *who only knows the loneliness*
smokestacks muted against a screaming blue timelessness
i produce only if she swallows she swallows only if i produce
in the window, i see myself transparent like a glass of milk drunk
down to a ghostly film the baby bigger, solidifies with every chug
and yet i'm filling up with something, a shadow cooling my uterus,
a red dress restitching itself

Breastfeeding the Museum of Fine Arts, Boston

Venus points her marble nipples
at everyone's mouths.

When my mother feeds me in the gallery,
a security guard ticks his finger, calls her forbidden.

I imagine the goddess turning to milk,
spilling her torso, splattering the floor.

One by one marble nymphs liquify.

My baby head becomes the moon
by which they tide. Our bench an island.

The guard grows small, his protestations adrift.

Milk dots appear on Tintaretto damsels.
The paint smudges, the bath-tub floods,

the angels abandon their corners to drink.
The painters turned off.

I drink my fill. I drink the marble, sip the paint.
Angels feed my mother grapes and goat.

She stands in the gallery like a performance artist.
See, this is life. This.

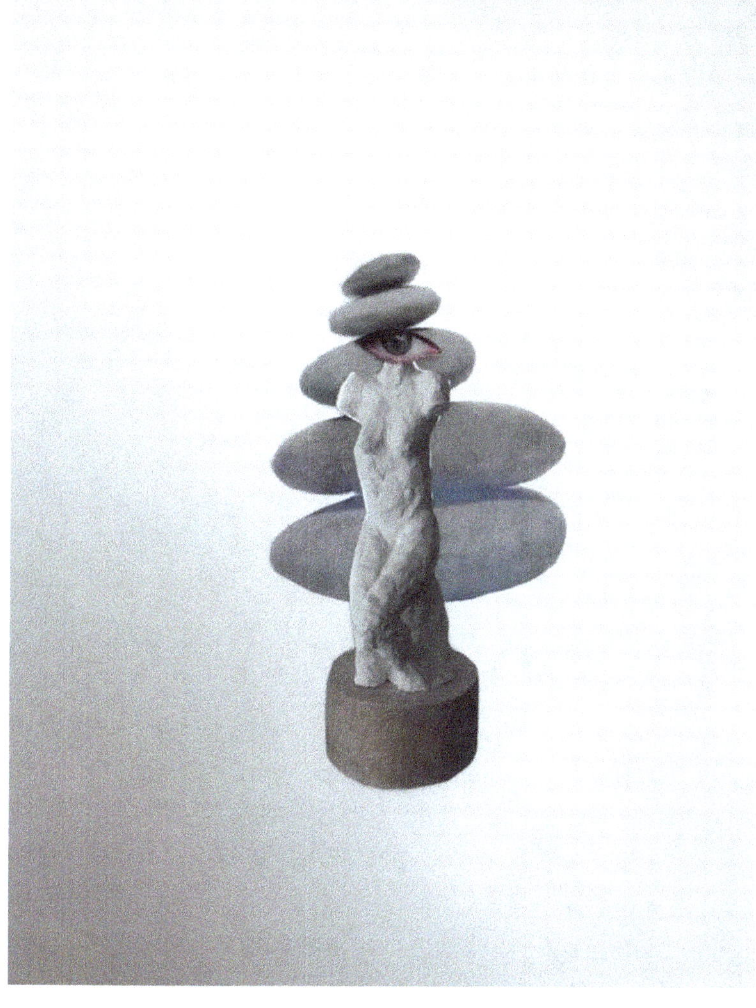

Acknowledgments

This book represents so many years of life and poetic community!
I am grateful to the Lesley University 2014 cohort and professors, and particularly to Cate Marvin, Steven Cramer, Teisha Twomey, Stephen Krauska, Heather Hughes, Stefan de Jesus Frias, Aimee Noel, Georgia Pearle Foster, and July Westhale.

To the writers from my Salem Writers Group days, in particular J.D. Scrimgeour, Jennifer Jean, Kevin Carey, Dawn Paul, Jennifer Martelli, Cindy Veach, Colleen Michaels, and January O'Neil, for their insights, interpretations, and the years of poetry community which has sustained and instructed me.

To Dave and Walnut Street Café in Lynn for giving me the seed of what became my manuscript – reading for twenty minutes gave me the push to find an arc, which eventually morphed into this book.

I'm grateful for my residency at The Home School, where I felt permission was granted to embrace the experimentation that calls to me and where new ways of working were illuminated. A special thank you to Douglas Kearney, Adam Fitzgerald, Emily Skillings, Annie Bielski, Henk Rousseau, and Jayna Schwartzman.

The Boom Zoom room, who helped me keep poetry alive during quarantine and while I was a new mother, trying to find time to finish a manuscript. Thanks Stephanie Angelini, Erica Charis-Molling, and all the other friends who flitted in and out to talk poetry.

Thanks to Joey Gould for being my partner in poetic shenanigans, always.

To Sarah Joy and Jessica Lynne Furtado, thank you for being my art witch sisters.

I'm grateful for PSNY and my Poetry Brothel crew. Thanks for being the weirdos I need in the world and giving me a space to play, perform, and experience poetry in new ways, to explore my fascination with persona and the personal.

I will be forever grateful to Eileen Cleary and Christine Jones for believing in this book, for their editorial precision and generosity, and for the wonderful community of writers they tirelessly shepherd through Lily Poetry Review and Lily Poetry Review Books.

To Mom and Dad for encouraging me to follow my passion for the arts and for bringing me up on stories, crossword puzzles, and cultural adventuring. To Grandpa Jerry for being such an important example of a professional artist to me as a child, and to all of my ancestors whose art practice has been handed down for me to continue.

To Juniper for offering me chances to play and to reawaken my curiosity about the world every day.

To Erik, always, for your partnership, for sharing the weight, for our beautiful life, for understanding when I morph it into warped exhibits of exclamation.

Exhibit: 7/11 appeared as Clerks in *Advice from a Siren,* a chapbook published by Dancing Girl Press in 2016.

Exhibits: 13, 10, 21, 30, and 27 were published as one poem by *Listen to Your Skin* in the *Listen to Your Skin Anthology,* winter 2024.

Thanks to *Painted Bride Quarterly* for publishing The Female Gaze series: Lee Miller, Frida Kahlo, and Laura Mulvey in Issue 100 and for discussing them on their podcast, *The Slush Pile,* episode 88.

The Female Gaze: Faith Ringgold appeared in *Sinister Wisdom* #125.

Escape to Swan Lake; the Man-Hunt Scene appeared in *Blue Lyra Review.*

The Moon Moth Lives for a Week after Emerging and Tender Garden appeared in *Drunk Monkeys* in March of 2017.

Pennsylvania Wedding was published by *Angime,* 2019.

The Artist appeared in *Paper Nautilus,* 2013.

Limnologist was published by *Lily Poetry Review,* Issue 7.

Traveler's Pledge was published by *Nixes Mate* Issue 28/29.

Pandemic Mother in the Window is forthcoming in *MER* Volume 22.

The Female Gaze: Tippi Hedren was published as Look Out in *Drunk Monkeys* October 2023 by Marginalia Publishing.

Titania the Sexbot Wakes in the Bower of the Interweb is a remix of Titania's monologue in "A Midsummer Night's Dream," Act III, scene i.

Canary, Velvet Cloud, and Glide are erasures of Hans Christian Anderson's "The Little Mermaid."

For The Female Gaze series, I began by creating erasures from the letters of Frida Kahlo, from Laura Mulvey's essay "The Male Gaze," and from an interview with Faith Ringgold, as well as employing ekphrasis on the works of Frida Kahlo, Lee Miller, Laura Mulvey, and Faith Ringgold.

The handcut collages appearing throughout are by the poet.

About the author

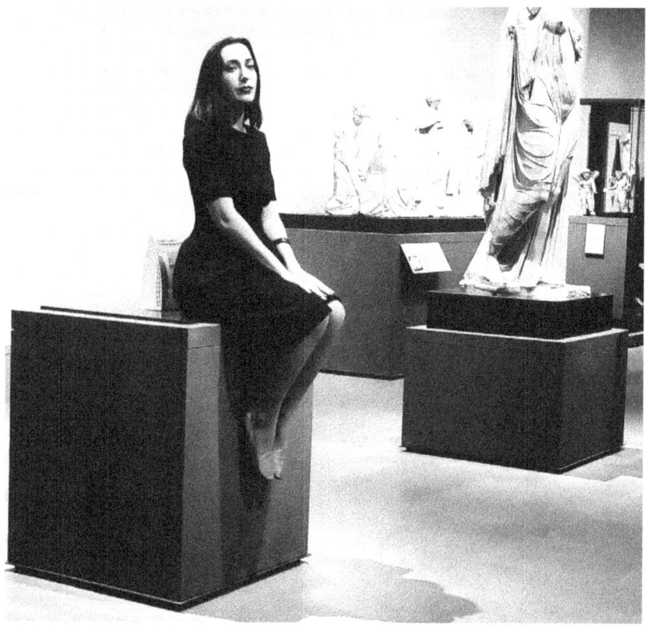

Shari Caplan (she/her) is a poet, actor, and event producer with a
passion for enlivening our collective imaginative potential. She's the
author of *The Red Shoes; a Phantasmagoric Ballet on Paper* (Lambhouse
Books, 2023), and *Advice from a Siren* (Dancing Girl Press, 2016).
A wearer of many tophats, she has produced and performed in "The
Poetry Circus," "The Fairy Tale Poetry Walking Tour," and other
cross-pollinations, including the Boston chapter of The Poetry
Brothel, an international immersive cabaret series (founded by The
Poetry Society of New York). Shari's work has appeared in *Gulf Coast,
Painted Bride Quarterly, Sinister Wisdom, Grimoire, Angime, Drunk
Monkeys,* and others and has earned her a scholarship to The Home
School in Hudson and a fellowship to The Vermont Studio Center,
as well as nominations for a Bettering American Poetry Award, a
Pushcart Prize, and a Rhylsing Award. She graduated with an MFA
from Lesley University in 2014. Find her work, workshops, monthly
love letter to creativity, and upcoming events at ShariCaplan.com.

www.ingramcontent.com/pod-product-compliance
Lightning Source LLC
Chambersburg PA
CBHW051814050726
47598CB00006B/2556